KU-002-290

PHILADELPHIA DISCOVERED

PHILADELPHIA DISCOVERED

Photographed by JOSEPH NETTIS   Introduction by NATHANIEL BURT

Published by
GREATER PHILADELPHIA MAGAZINE

FIRST EDITION

COPYRIGHT 1964 IN ALL COUNTRIES IN THE
INTERNATIONAL COPYRIGHT UNION BY
GREATER PHILADELPHIA MAGAZINE
PHILADELPHIA, PA., U.S.A.

ALL RIGHTS RESERVED
EDITORIAL SUPERVISION BY ALAN HALPERN
BOOK DESIGN BY HUBERT KAHANA

PRINTED IN PHILADELPHIA BY THE BECK ENGRAVING COMPANY

LIBRARY OF CONGRESS CATALOG CARD NUMBER 64-24727

Contents

Introduction

A big city: larger than Boston or Denver or Detroit or San Francisco; larger than Seattle and Portland put together; larger than New Orleans or Washington or Miami or Memphis. Larger in fact than any American cities except New York and Chicago and, until just recently, Los Angeles. Larger than any cities of England or France or Spain or Italy except their capitals, London, Paris, Madrid, Rome. Larger than Vienna, larger than Budapest, larger than Amsterdam or Rotterdam, Singapore or Warsaw, Istanbul or Stockholm, Lisbon or Havana. In fact only a dozen or so world cities, most of them capitals, the boom cities of South America, or the pullulating cities of the Orient, have as great a metropolitan population. Philadelphia has been called the largest provincial city in the world. Philadelphians, over two million within the city limits, over four million if one includes the suburbs outside, are almost as numerous as the Danes or the Swiss.

The size of a city can be measured in other things besides mere population. The six million inhabitants of Los Angeles have still failed to make a real city of it. There is a weight and feeling of power about Philadelphia itself that make it a big city. The heavy grandeur of City Hall at the center of Philadelphia's conservative skyline, the grand sweep out from it of Broad and Market Streets and the Benjamin Franklin Parkway, this concentration of skyscrapers at the center and these avenues of escape outward immediately give an impression of a sort of spaciousness and grandeur. Impressive: an atmosphere halfway between New York—skyscrapers, metropolitan busyness—and Washington—vistas and columns. And of course Philadelphia is, in fact, geographically right between them.

These skyscrapers represent power, too. The great Philadelphia banks are still among the oldest and most prosperous in the nation. The Pennsylvania Railroad whose pillared 30th Street Station closes the vista of the new John F. Kennedy Boulevard as the Art Museum does that of the older Parkway, still remains the "World's Greatest Railroad" and a Philadelphia-based affair. Philadelphia institutions, in which she takes such pride, the Academy of Music, "The Old Lady of Locust Street" that houses the world-famed Philadelphia Orchestra, the Free Library and the Franklin Institute and the Pennsylvania Academy of Fine Arts, the University of Pennsylvania and the Museum of Art are all first of their kind.

John Wanamaker's, Philadelphia's own store with its stories-high courtyard and renowned pipe organ and Christmas displays, still offers its ever-faithful customers everything they could want. The kind of financial and shopping and cultural superiority that makes a city worthwhile is nowhere more impressively and conveniently concentrated than in Philadelphia's central city, that area from the Delaware to the Schuylkill on either side of Market Street. Philadelphia is a great port; the Delaware River complex as a whole is the second largest shipping center in the nation. It is a great manufacturing area, electronics and steel and paper and textiles and drugs. Philadelphia is the focal point of a great railroad complex.

This is all true enough; Philadelphia is big all right, and rich and busy. So are other cities. This is not what makes Philadelphia special, different.

Philadelphia is a small city: this is what makes it special. For all the huge body of it, the population and all the statistics of size and worth, it is a very intimate place. Other cities, too, can boast of tonnages and capital and votes delivered. But nobody can call Chicago or New York or Los Angeles or Detroit "cosy." Philadelphia is cosy. Even at the very center of the city, at the corner of Broad and Chestnut Streets, people keep running into each other, casually, without surprise. I once stood for a noonday hour at this, the most crowded corner of the city, the combination of Philadelphia's Wall Street (finance) and Fifth Avenue (shopping). Not only did I see several familiar faces myself, but this greeting of friends, people of every kind and age, was commonplace. One man, obviously a bank executive, strolled along meditatively, twiddling his glasses in one hand. Nobody in Wall Street would dare to stroll, much less hold his glasses like that. They'd be knocked down and trampled in the lunch-hour rush. Scarcely more than a block away from this core of the city's shopping and financial life lie little residential streets left over from the old Philadelphia of red brick and white marble steps. Once fashionable, then slums, and now bought up and made pretty again, a whole network of picturesque backwaters parallels the shopping streets from river to river—Waverly and Addison and Panama and Ringgold and Camac and Quince and Iseminger and Clinton; oldest of all, Elfreth's Alley near the Delaware, dating back to the time of William Penn. One can spend weeks poking in and out of such nooks and crannies. In them lies the essence of Old Philadelphia charm: sleepy, bosky, and above all—cosy.

This cosiness extends outwards, north, south, west into innumerable neighborhoods, each with its own pride and character: the old Negro section along and below South Street, which has been a Negro section almost since Philadelphia began, the Italian section below that, which still produces opera and pop singers and maintains an Italian street market, and below that a neighborhood called the Neck, whose natives, called Neckers, are supposed to talk with a special accent all their own. It is from the neighborhoods of South Philadelphia that the Mummers' Parade, that mysterious Philadelphia folk festival, originates. Thousands belong to clubs with names like Golden Sunrise, Liberty Clowns, Ferko and Hog Island. There they meet all year long in their club houses to fabricate the gorgeous, silly costumes they wear in the New Year's Mummers' Parade up Broad Street.

North Philadelphia is equally neighborhoody and has its special character. Remnants of past glory, the millionaire mansions of the Wideners and others, the fine Victorian temples of 19th-century Jewish gentry, still crop out here and there along North Broad. There is a region along the river called the Bend, whose natives are Benders, to correspond with South Philadelphia's Neckers. Also along the river is Kensington, still populated by the descendants of English textile workers who came here in the mid-19th century. It was they who made cricket Philadelphia's great game. From the Civil War to the First World War everybody, rich and poor, played and watched cricket in Philadelphia, and belonged to cricket clubs. Now such cricket clubs as are left have become tennis clubs. But everybody belongs to some sort of club, or association or fraternal order or layman's religious society. The Pyramid Club in North Philadelphia is the country's most exclusive Negro club, the Catholic Philopatrian Institute, once a fiery Irish debating society, is the stronghold of old Catholic families, the Union League, squatting on South Broad in General Grant insolence and period charm, is the center of Republican politics. Once no Democrat was allowed to pass the door, and old-line Southern Democrat families crossed to the other side of Broad Street to avoid walking in front of it. Everybody belongs to a club in Philadelphia, everybody belongs to a neighborhood, everybody belongs to a family. It is this universal webbing of connections that makes Philadelphia a small town. It can make a newcomer, who doesn't yet belong, seem like the new kid at a birthday party—or the Victorian waif with his nose pressed against the windowpane on Christmas Eve. But for the natives, or those absorbed into native life, there is little of that dreadful anonymity, that feeling of being a lost atom in a fissionable universe that attacks the dwellers in those big cities that are nothing but big.

Size and intimacy, power and cosiness—it is the combination that gives Philadelphia its special character. Other cities, smaller cities, are cosy too. Other cities, larger cities, are powerful; but none just right in the middle as is this middle city of the Middle Atlantic States, both great *and* cosy.

These two poles of Philadelphia's character, cosiness and greatness, are aptly represented by Philadelphia's two great men, William Penn, the Quaker founder, and Benjamin Franklin, the Revolutionary leader. No other American city is dominated in quite the same way by two such individuals. Boston owes her foundation and qualities to Puritanism, rather than to any one Puritan, New York to the Dutch, not any one Dutchman. Even Providence, that owes so much to Roger Williams, has no similarly all-important Revolutionary figure. Not only are the two great Philadelphians memorialized physically in conspicuous ways—the statue of William Penn stands on the very top of the tower of City Hall, still the highest thing in all the city, the biggest bridge to New Jersey is called the Benjamin Franklin Bridge, and the great esplanade northwestward, the Benjamin Franklin Parkway— but the spirits of Penn and Franklin still operate in Philadelphia in dozens of ways.

Philadelphia's greatness and the greatness of its institutions are almost directly the legacy of Franklin. Never has one man done so much for his adopted home town. You can start at Independence Hall, now a National Park as well as a national shrine (Philadelphians prefer to call it the "State House"). Franklin did not have a hand in building it, but he spent endless days inside the building, a notable signer of the Declaration of Independence, one of the principal agents, later on, in moulding the Constitution. Next door to the State House, almost joining it on Fifth Street, is an institution that Franklin definitely did found: the Philosophical

Society, America's oldest and most distinguished scientific organization. Almost every scientist of note in America, from Philadelphia's Benjamin Franklin, the "discoverer of electricity," to Princeton's Albert Einstein, the "discoverer of relativity," has been a member. Across the street is a new building, an exact replica of an old one. This is the library of the Philosophical Society; but it is a copy of the old Library Company's building, that of America's first subscription and public library—founded by Benjamin Franklin. The statue of the founder over the doorway was said to come down every evening at five o'clock and head for the nearest saloon. Westward a few blocks stand the fine old buildings of the Pennsylvania Hospital, oldest hospital in the nation and, of course, founded by Benjamin Franklin. On every other brick house one sees little lead plaques, insurance markers. Many have the symbol on them of four clasped hands. This indicates that the house is or was insured by America's first fire insurance company, the Philadelphia Contributionship for the Insurance of Houses from Loss by Fire, founded by—Benjamin Franklin. The Contributionship, once so conservative that it was said to insure only pig iron under high water mark, has an old office building, looking like a good men's club, just south of Independence Hall on Fourth Street. Out on Benjamin Franklin Parkway sits the Franklin Institute, wonderful push-button museum of mechanical devices and models. The building, though a 20th-century one, was actually built in part with Franklin's own money, a fund he created to be saved up, increased and used by the city for a worthy cause. Farther out, in West Philadelphia, there sprawls the increasingly elaborate campus of the great University of Pennsylvania. Need you ask who founded it? Benjamin Franklin, of course.

This only begins the list of Philadelphia institutions, universities and museums, not all of course actually founded by Franklin. Besides "the University" (for many Philadelphians there is only one "University") there are a dozen others such as Temple, Drexel Institute, the Catholic colleges: Villanova, St. Joseph's and La Salle, the Quaker colleges: Bryn Mawr, Haverford and Swarthmore.

Most conspicuous of all Philadelphia institutions, and one of which Philadelphians grow increasingly and justifiably proud, is the Museum of Art, visible from any direction on its rocky hill, once the site of a reservoir, at the end of the Parkway.

It has nothing to do with Franklin, but it houses one of the country's great art collections, and along with the more archaeological University Museum, the Academy of Fine Arts, oldest of America's art schools, the Rodin Museum, and the Fleisher Collection, down in South Philadelphia, it helps make Philadelphia an outstanding center of the fine arts. The Barnes Collection, out in suburban Merion, assembled by the cantankerous drug manufacturer Dr. Albert Barnes, is considered the finest collection of modern French art in the country.

Philadelphia is especially proud of its institutions, and proud of Franklin for having started so many of them; but Franklin, as well as being a founder, a scientist, a statesman and a writer, was a businessman too. Philadelphia insurance, now represented by huge modern companies like the Penn Mutual on Independence Square, and the Insurance Company of North America on the Parkway, could also be considered a descendant of Franklin's first company, the Contributionship. Printing and publishing, the business where Franklin got his start and made his fortune, have been famous Philadelphia businesses too. But alas, the most conspicuous landmark of Philadelphia publishing, the Curtis Publishing Company with its devious connections with Franklin through The Saturday Evening Post, is no longer a Philadelphia company. Its offices still dominate Independence Square westward, but the magazines are edited in New York.

Financial and industrial Philadelphia can hardly be said to date from Franklin. Manufacturing began before Franklin arrived, and banking in Philadelphia dates from the Revolution with Robert Morris who more than any one man helped finance American independence. For decades Philadelphia remained the banking center of the United States, and some of the oldest bank buildings, the Girard Bank on Dock Street and Nicholas Biddle's Bank of the United States, are preserved as architectural monuments in the National Park area down near Independence Hall. A long line of Philadelphia bankers, Robert Morris, Stephen Girard, Nicholas Biddle, Francis Drexel, Jay Cooke, have left their mark on the city. It is significant that whereas in other cities the skyline is often as not dominated by the buildings of commercial companies, such old worthies in New York as the Singer and Woolworth and Chrysler buildings for instance, Philadelphia's skyline is predominantly one of banks and insurance companies.

That does not mean that Philadelphia is not industrial; north and south along the Delaware River from the U.S. Steel mills near Trenton down past Du Pont in Wilmington stretches an almost continuous line of factories. Over in Camden are the huge plants of Campbell Soup and RCA, originally the Victor Talking Machine Company, for whom Caruso made Red Seal Records. Southward lie the refinery and shipyards of the Pew family and the headquarters of Scott Paper.

Philadelphia's oldest manufacturers were up Philadelphia's other river, the Schuylkill. The remains of the Rittenhouse paper mill of 1690 can still be seen on one of its tributaries, the Wissahickon, now in Fairmount Park. Old companies, like the Alan Wood Steel Company, still operate in picturesque Schuylkill River milltowns like Manayunk, Norristown and Conshohocken.

If Philadelphia's institutional and intellectual world is "founded by Benjamin Franklin," Philadelphia's basic workaday and stay-at-home world is founded by William Penn. Franklin is involved in most of the things that tourists want to see, including his own severely simple tomb in old Christ Church graveyard. But Penn created the city itself, and much of its character is due to him and to his Quaker followers. Franklin made public Philadelphia, Penn private Philadelphia.

Not only did Penn found the colony, but he also planned the layout of the city. He determined the gridiron plan of it, with four parks symmetrically arranged, now named after Logan, Penn's secretary and a scientist; Rittenhouse, Philadelphia's 18-century astronomer; Washington and Franklin. In the middle was another square, now filled up by the bulk of City Hall. Philadelphia was the first of America's big cities to be laid out at right angles, a device so simple that it has been adopted as the norm of city plans in America, but without the saving grace of the little squares. Penn's plan went further than this, however. He also planned the countryside around the city, and one can still follow country roads laid out in straight lines by Penn's 17th-century surveyors.

He reserved the lands north and south of his gridiron central city for the so-called "Liberties." These were set aside as suburban developments. His idea was that city folk should have country interests, and to that end the buyers of city lots were given large lots in the Liberties, or country farms farther out. This balance of country and city has persisted to this day. Philadelphia is still the suburban city par excellence; more than half its real population now lives outside the city limits, and from the very beginning Philadelphia's well-to-do had country places as well as city houses.

Philadelphia is not exactly the green country town Penn hoped it would turn out to be; but it still has more trees in it than any other American big city except Washington, largely because it has Fairmount Park. This, the biggest American park within city limits, was once all country estates along the salubrious Schuylkill. The building of a dam across the river brought mosquitoes, and drove away the rich owners. The city forehandedly bought up the deserted estates, and that was the beginning of the park. Many of the old estate houses are still there, preserved now as museums. It is possible to walk right from City Hall to the farthest reaches of Chestnut Hill and so into the country via the Parkway, Fairmount Park and the Wissahickon without ever passing through a real, unshaded city street.

Part of Penn's legacy is this countrified atmosphere. The most characteristic view of the Philadelphia skyline is still that across the rolling meadows and high trees of the Park. A suburban fondness for trees, gardens and lawns, and a continuous interest in outdoor sports have always been part of the Philadelphia make-up. Penn himself was a dashing fox hunter in his youth, and from the founding of the colony to the present, Quaker fox hunters have been a by-product of this Philadelphia city-country life. There are still fox hunts all around the edges of the city, though they are continually being driven farther out by the sprawl of developments. Tennis, in Fairmount Park and elsewhere, also flourishes in this atmosphere of trees and grass. During the twenties Philadelphia produced gentlemen-amateur tennis champions like Big Bill Tilden. The dam across the Schuylkill created calm water and a place to row, and in turn created rowing champions like Jack Kelly, who got his training there. The rowing clubs, called "barge clubs," line the river near the Art Museum, across from the Pennsylvania Railroad tracks and that other ornament of Philadelphia's great Park, the beloved Zoo, first of its kind in the country.

Charitable Philadelphia is also a Quaker legacy. Sometimes sports and charity got mixed up, as in a fine old institution called the Skating and Humane Society. It was once an organization set up to rescue people who fell through the ice when skating on the Schuylkill in winter. Now it is just a private skating club. Besides founding almshouses and reforming prisons, the Quakers founded many of Philadelphia's best secondary schools like the venerable Penn Charter, which is still run by a 17th-century-founded Quaker Board of Overseers; though not many of the students there are Friends these days. Quakers did not found colleges in the early days, since they had no ministry that needed training. Later on, however, they gave in; and now the three Quaker colleges, all-female Bryn Mawr, all-male Haverford and coeducational Swarthmore, are three of the most internationally famous of smaller colleges.

The most important legacy of Penn was religious tolerance. From the very beginning all religions and sects were allowed to worship openly. At a time when the British government looked on Catholics as potential traitors, the way the American government now looks on Communists, Philadelphia was the only 18th-century city in the whole British Empire where mass could be celebrated publicly. From the beginning of the colony, Jews were encouraged and accepted, and for generations the leading Jewish families were leaders of society too. All the various Christian denominations have deep roots in the city, and still today a basic acknowledgment of the rights of minorities and of freedom of belief underlies the city's psychology.

As Philadelphia is a "City of Churches" it is also a "City of Homes." Philadelphia's architecture, as well as its city plan, seems to have been created by Quakers. Whereas New Englanders early adopted the free-standing frame house, usually white-painted, Philadelphians took to low brick houses flush to the street and connected to each other, a plan of building derived from the English towns from which the first Quaker immigrants came. Even in small Pennsylvania villages this pattern persisted, and in the 19th century developed, after the model of London, into the brick rowhouse, curse or blessing of the city, depending on how well the houses are built. In earlier days, when the houses were well proportioned and prettily faced with shutters, fan-lit doors and white marble steps, nothing was more serenely modest and comfortable than a Quaker street of Philadelphia brick rowhouses. Later in the 19th century the rowhouses were thrown up without benefit of architect or taste, and nothing can be more dreary now than a dingy, monotonous, treeless, shutterless street of rundown cheap rowhouses. The principle of home ownership, of occupancy of each house by its single family, was established, so that in contradistinction to Manhattan with its apartments and tenements, Philadelphia still tends to be a city of homeowners. A good many apartments have now been built and are now building, but old-time Philadelphians look on them with disapproval; and in fact they are certainly violations of the whole spirit and character of the city.

This basic spirit and character still retains something of the Quaker—cautious, conservative, tolerant, laborious, full of a belief in privacy and quietness. Manners are relaxed, unlike the rest of the North, but never flowery, as in the South. Philadelphians are willing to be pleasant to strangers, but they are not very interested in them. They don't like to be asked questions by outsiders and usually react with a sort of bewilderment. Everybody in Boston knows just where everything is, though he's often quite wrong. You have to persist to get a direction out of a Philadelphian. The story of the traveler in Pennsylvania Dutch country is representative. He asked a native for the way to the Pretzel Factory. "I dunno," was the answer. Just as the stranger was pulling away, the native dashed after him. "You mean the *Pretzel* Factory?" "Yes." "Oh. Well, I dunno."

Modesty in houses, in clothes, in conversation is characteristic too. Philadelphians as a rule don't trust a woman who is *too* well dressed. She might be from New York. Among themselves they spend a great deal of time disparaging the city, its weather, its politics, its street cleaning department, and any modern changes. But an outsider shouldn't make the mistake of joining in: this indoor sport of disparagement is for natives only. Philadelphians seem almost happy when one of their local teams, baseball or football, is at the bottom of the league (where they so often are). It gives them a wonderful excuse to grouse. But the great days of Connie Mack when Philadelphia baseball ruled the roost are still remembered fondly.

Philadelphians also are often the first to run down their own restaurants and night clubs and theatres. After all, a good dinner at home with family and friends is more to Philadelphia's taste than eating out with a lot of perfect strangers. Still, despite all the bad publicity, there are lots of good places to eat in Philadelphia. No sea food is better than that found at picturesque Bookbinder's, down near the Delaware, or Italian food than that found at Dante's and Luigi's down in South Philadelphia. No hotel restaurants are more elegant than those of the Barclay or the Warwick or the Bellevue. Theatres and a few scattered night clubs do a thriving business and bring to Philadelphia all the stars and headliners of the nation.

But public life is not really the area Philadelphians prefer. They do not tend to live on the streets as do Parisians or Neapolitans, or even New Yorkers. Philadelphia streets are pretty much deserted at midnight. Like Londoners, Philadelphians prefer to retire to their rowhouses, or plant daffodils in suburban gardens. Despite all modern improvements (or disturbances), Philadelphia remains the City of Homes.

For all this native hominess, reserve and conservatism, all that is old or even dingy about Philadelphia, no stranger can fail to observe that extraordinary things are going on. As the businessman drives from the station to his hotel he can hardly avoid seeing the new buildings about City Hall. If he stays longer, he will discover that every part of the city is full of this same fever of construction and reconstruction. All very odd for a place that has prided itself for so long on being stand pat and even stick-in-the-mud.

These changes are the by-products of something known locally as the "Philadelphia Renaissance." No picture of Philadelphia would be complete without some reference to this event, the most exciting thing in the city's career since the Centennial Exhibition of 1876. The truth is that beginning about 1920 Philadelphia began to slip down hill. The bases of Philadelphia's 19th-century prosperity, particularly railroads and coal, were becoming obsolete. The depression of the thirties hit an economy that was already receding. The depression, that in New York under La Guardia stirred up a reform, merely caused Philadelphia to sink deeper into disrepair. The Republican administration refused to accept any Federal aid from a Democratic national regime, and had no money to do anything on its own.

Though the end of the depression and the boom of the Second War helped a bit, Philadelphia by 1950 was becalmed and disintegrating.

Then came the revolution. In 1952 under the leadership of Joseph Sill Clark, later to become Senator from Pennsylvania, and Richardson Dilworth, both of whom were elected mayor, the ancient and corrupt administration in City Hall was thrown out. A new charter and a new government infused new life into the old city. A plan for more or less remodeling the whole city, tearing down slums, preserving old shrines, was put into effect. Institutions like the University of Pennsylvania and Temple University took on a new lease of life and began to expand in every direction. Philadelphia was stirred up like an ant hill.

The most conspicuous results of this new order are the two developments known as Penn Center and Society Hill. The railroad viaduct that once cut the city in two just north of Market Street, aptly nicknamed the "Chinese Wall," was torn down and a boulevard put in its place. West of City Hall a plaza with business buildings scattered about in it, Penn Center, has made a new "downtown" for city business life. About it apartments, hotels and garages have clustered, running along Kennedy Boulevard towards 30th Street Station. If all the construction that is planned finally gets completed, the Boulevard will provide a sort of very modern, sleek, white Triumphal Entrance to the city, leading straight from the station to the very center. Quite a change from the old Philadelphia of Quaker brick rowhouses.

Society Hill, down by the Delaware, is different. Here is an attempt to salvage what is good of the old and combine it with modernity. Hundreds of beautiful old houses that had degenerated into slums have been bought by private owners and remodeled. Around them the disfiguring warehouses and garages have been torn down and in the empty spaces new buildings—tall apartments, low modern town houses—or green gardens and walkways have been planned; in fact, already exist. As City Hall is the focal point for the Penn Center development, so Independence Hall is the focal point for Society Hill. Though far from completed, the plan is quickly taking shape. When the Bicentennial of 1976 comes around, Society Hill should be a dream world of the old and the new. Philadelphia won't have to build a fair to celebrate; it can simply show off the city itself.

These two projects, Penn Center and Society Hill, are only two of dozens of other planning projects, ranging from the refurbishing of City Hall and the old Academy of Music to a gigantic "City of Science" out in West Philadelphia bordering the University and nearby Drexel Institute. Experiments in slum clearance and slum up-grading covering many square miles, facilities like the new Food Center in South Philadelphia, highways like the Schuylkill Expressway—these and countless other improvements are signs of the new spirit that has galvanized the city. Philadelphia, no longer "corrupt" or "contented" as it was called in muckraking days, has been lifting itself up out of the doldrums, remaking itself, restoring itself. The spirit of Benjamin Franklin seems to be stirring again, after a long sleep.

The spirit of William Penn, however, the Quakerism of Philadelphia, still prevails, calm, tolerant, cautious, quiet and home-loving. For all the new apartments, Philadelphia clings to red brick and rowhouse. In the countrified reaches of Fairmount Park, the great surrounding bushy miles of suburbs, Philadelphians take their ease, tend their flowers and play their games. In endless wards of the city itself Philadelphians join their associations, support their varied houses of worship, gossip about their friends and pride themselves on being just a bit different and better than the strangers in neighborhoods a few blocks away. They continue to grouse about the climate, the street cleaning department and the standing of the local ball teams. They love to run Philadelphia down; but they wouldn't dream of living anywhere else. Whatever they may say about their city, those that live there love it. Perhaps a book like this one may show some of the reasons why.

Nathaniel Burt

Most big cities sprawl at the center but Philadelphia's downtown is compressed—snugly nestled between two rivers. Shops and offices cluster conveniently around City Hall. People in town seldom take taxis; it's almost as easy to stroll. Philadelphia is built on a human scale. The streets are narrow and easy to cross. Buildings rise but they don't tower. And when the pavements close in, the green oases of Washington and Rittenhouse Squares are only a few steps away. And everywhere there is variety: The skyscraper that's barely a few months old, the department store that's pure Victorian gingerbread, the insurance company headquarters that's older than the country. You never know what's around the next corner

Center City

←Girard Trust Bank, Broad and Chestnut

City Hall, from Parkway

Union Leagu

The Automat

doorman

Views along Market Street

JESUS
SAVES
CHARLIE & JACKS
BETTER CLOTHING
SAVE 240 5 7 9 SAVE
SHOES
CLOTHING
SAVE
WORK & DRESS CLOTHES
230
Square Deal at Charlie's & Jack's
Carhartt
NO PARKING
8AM-6PM
EXCEPT SUNDAY
SUMMER ST.
STOP
SAVE 357
234
236

Antique shop, Market Street

Pet shop, Penn Center

Polynesian restaurant, Walnut Street

Penn Center through City Hall arch

←Central court, John Wanamaker's

Department store Sa

Christmas lights, Chestnut Street

Canadian pipers in City Hall courtyard

ench sailor on leave   Pretzel vendor

Women's
specialty sho
Walnut Stree

Window shopping, Chestnut Street

play house statue, Arch Street

Burlesque house dancer, Arch Street

49

← New Year's parade, Chinatown

Fire marker

Society Hill

Delancey Street

St. James Place

Rittenhouse Square

Parkway statuary

Midnight, West Penn Squa

Market Street bookstore

Market Street →

65

GREGORY PECK
TONY CURTIS
FOX
TONY
CURTIS
CAPTAIN NEWMAN
STANTON
ORDER BRIDE
BUDDY EBSEN
DULLEA LOIS NETTLETON
AFFAIR
BOB HOPE
MICKEY SHAUGHNESSY
PENNY LAND
VOICE
RECORDING
DOCKTOR'S PET
POLICE

Strawberry Mansion Bridge

Fairmount Park

The pastoral presence of Fairmount Park relieves the long urban vistas of brick and asphalt. Over 7000 acres of wooded slopes, rolling meadows and open river make it the largest city park in the world. In some spots the park is as well manicured as a palace garden, in others it is wild and untouched. And threading it is the calm Schuylkill and its tributaries. By imposing a swath of countryside diagonally across Philadelphia, Fairmount Park welds it together rather than dividing it, lifting the whole city visually, and providing a vast and various playground for its citizens—a place where they can sport together, or separately contemplate the violets and the stars.

Conversation, near Parkside Avenue

Tete a tete, Lemon Hill

Statue, East River Drive

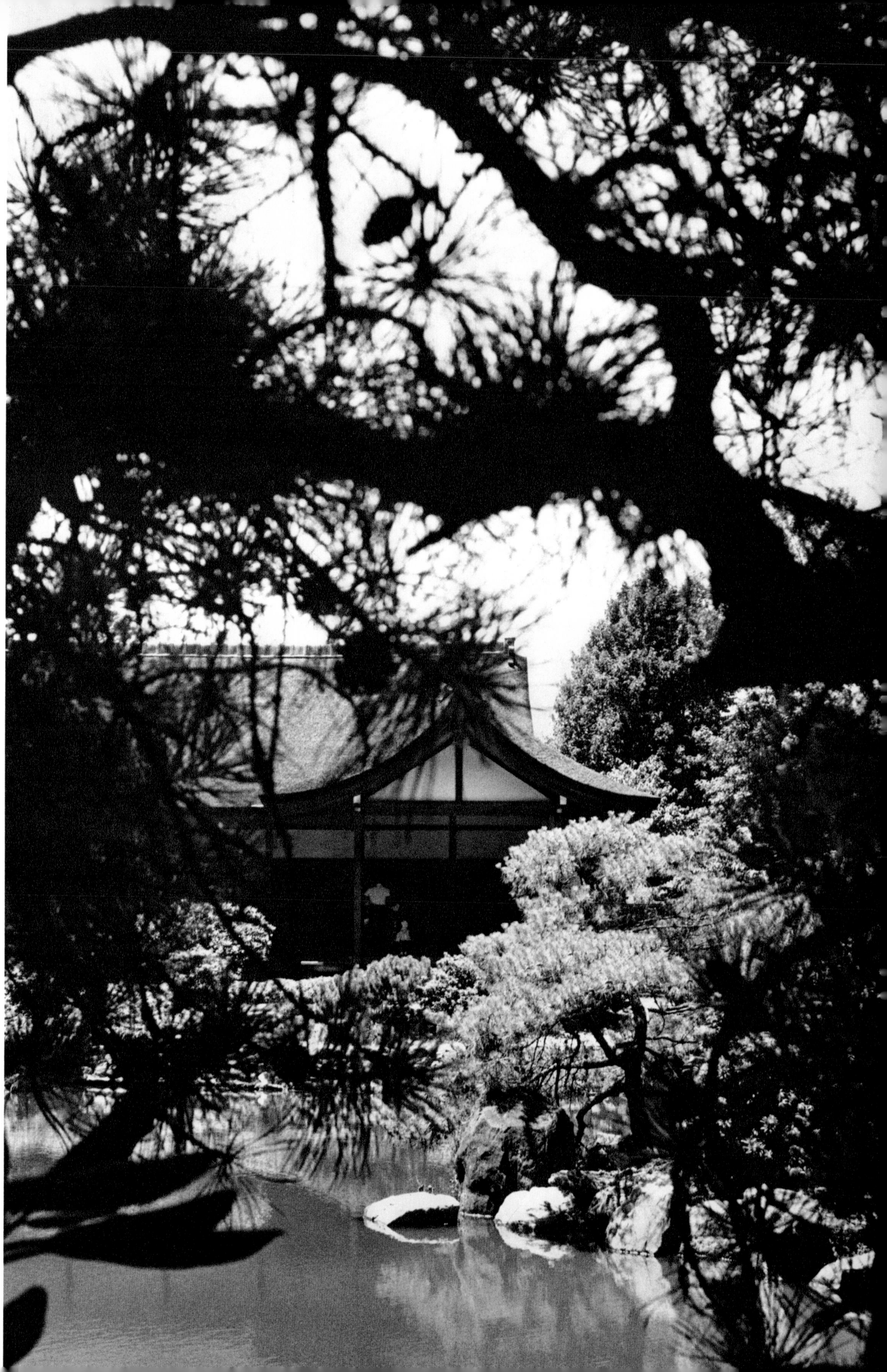

War memorial

Art Museum

ART MUSEUM
ANNENBERG,
McILHENNY, TYSC
and Other Collections
JULY 3 - SEPTEMBER
OPEN
WEEKDAYS
SUNDAY

Chess match, Strawberry Mansion

Bird watchers along upper Wissahickon

Artist at Art Mus

Folk dancing on Art Museum terrace

Fountain, East River Drive

←College scullers

Schuylkill Expressway

Park bridle path

Rented sailb

East bank of Schuylkill

Home-made rowboat

John B. Kelly Pool

Park league game

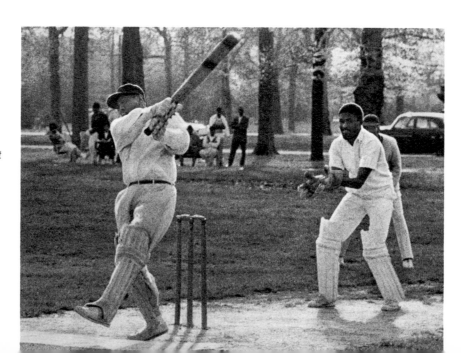

West Indians play cricket

Zoo bear pen

Wissahickon Creek

Valley Green

Trout season
opens in
the Wissahickon

← Covered bridge, upper Wissahickon

bin Hood Dell

Playhouse in the Park

Elevated train stop, West Philadelphia

The Neighborhoods

Ever since Penn landed on Philadelphia's waterfront, new settlers have followed in droves, leapfrogging their communities farther and farther out from the core. The current boundaries of the city go back to 1854. That was the year dozens of these tiny boroughs and townships were consolidated into one political entity. The old boundary lines may have been erased, but not the neighborhoods. Everybody in Philadelphia and its ever-lengthening suburbs belongs to a community. People don't say, "I'm from Philadelphia." They say, "I'm from Olney," or "I'm from Gulph Mills." After a while it becomes clear that Philadelphia is not a great, amorphous metropolis. It's really a collection of small towns.

ainian section, near Seventh and Girard

Manayunk

Society Hill apartment towers

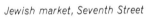

Jewish market, Seventh Street

Italian market, Ninth Street

Main Line mansion

Haverford Station, Main Line

←View down 34th Street
toward
Convention Hall

University
of Pennsylvania
dormitories

ROTC,
St. Joseph's College

ding party,
an Circle

uerto Rican
section,
rth Central
hiladelphia

Funeral at St. Francis Xavier

←— *Frank Lloyd Wright-designed synagogue, Elkins Park*

Schoolyard fight, Grays Fer

High school soccer team

Roxborough High School

Apartment tower, Parkway

Manayunk

Willow Grove Park

Southwark Plaza playground

Play area, South Philadelphia

Art Museum fountain

Independence Mall

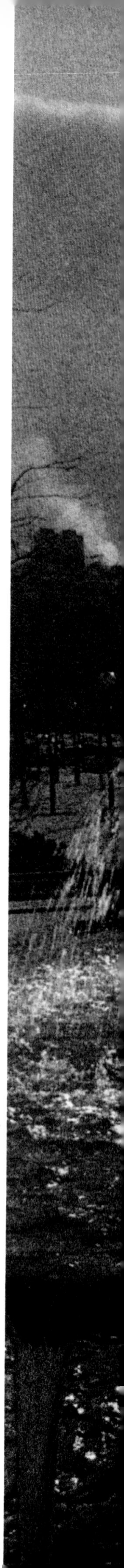

Flower show, Convention Hall

North Philadelphia intersection →

Apartment house, Parkway

Independence Hall

The colonial firebrands had to come to Philadelphia. For one thing, it was halfway between the hills of New Hampshire and the plains of Georgia. But, more important, it was *the* influential city—a city of energy and power, the commercial and intellectual crossroads of the New World. So to Philadelphia they came to discuss their grievances against the Crown, and, in 1776, to take the ultimate insurrectionary step. Today, the landmarks of this ancient affirmation of freedom still stand, somehow preserved through two centuries, their faded majesty painstakingly restored, their message just as meaningful as ever.

A Nation's Heritage

◀— *Liberty Bell*

Christ Church, interior

Cemet◦
Old St. Mary's Chu◦

Old Custom House, near Society Hill

Benjamin Franklin statue on Penn campus

Carpenters' Hall, near Society Hill

Wax Museum, off Independence Mall

Edgar Allan Poe's home

Market Square, Germantown

Head House, Society Hill

Quaker meeting house, Germantown

William Penn statue atop City Hall

Valley Forge

167

Oil refinery, Southwest Philadelphia

The Working Day

Philadelphia is huskier than it looks. You have to find the industry because most of it is tucked away, along the banks of the Delaware, neatly packaged in planned parks along the perimeter, in the back stretches of Kensington. But it's there and it's solid and, generally, it's been around for quite a long time. Philadelphia has always been a great port—it imports more cargo than any other city in the nation. It refines more oil than any other city but one. It pours steel. It builds railroad cars and it runs railroads. It makes giant electric dynamos and delicate electronic parts so small they're barely visible. Once a major textile center, it is now busy making hardware that's destined to tame space. And it never used to do that. At least, not since Franklin's kite.

el furnace stoker

Yard worker

Television stu

Metal salvager

← *Steel mill, Conshohocken*

Men's tailor

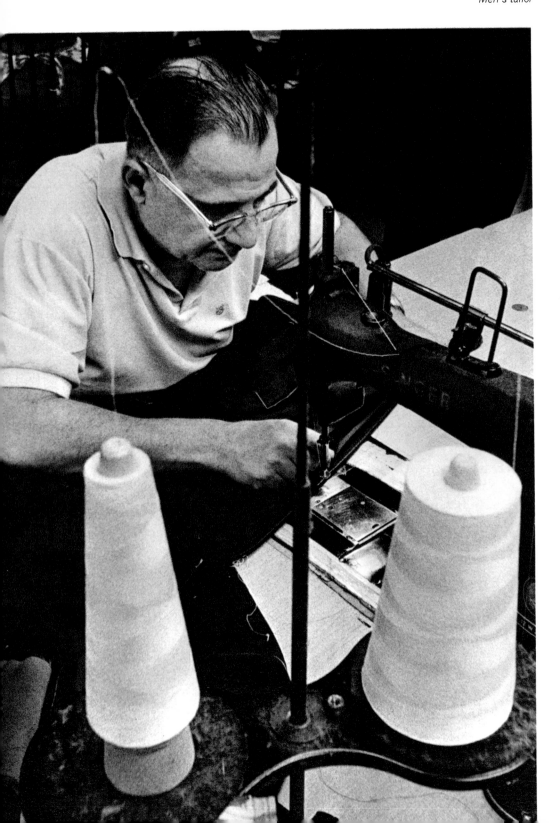

Magazine press room   Railroad signalman

←*Office workers, 15th Street*

Framework of Delaware Expressway

Benjamin Franklin Bridge

←— Ore unloading pier, Port Richmond

Municipal pier, South Philadelphia

Paper warehouse

Food Distribution Center

International Airport →

Reading Terminal Market

Industrial
model
maker

Pharmace
res
sci

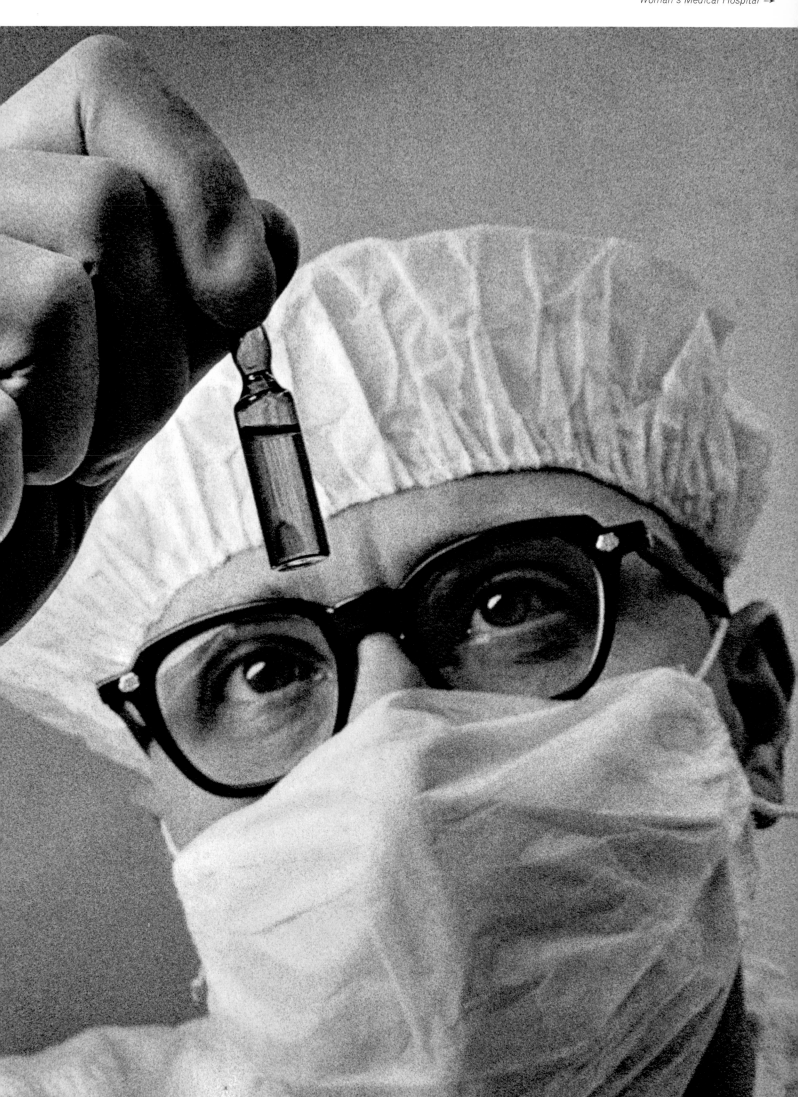

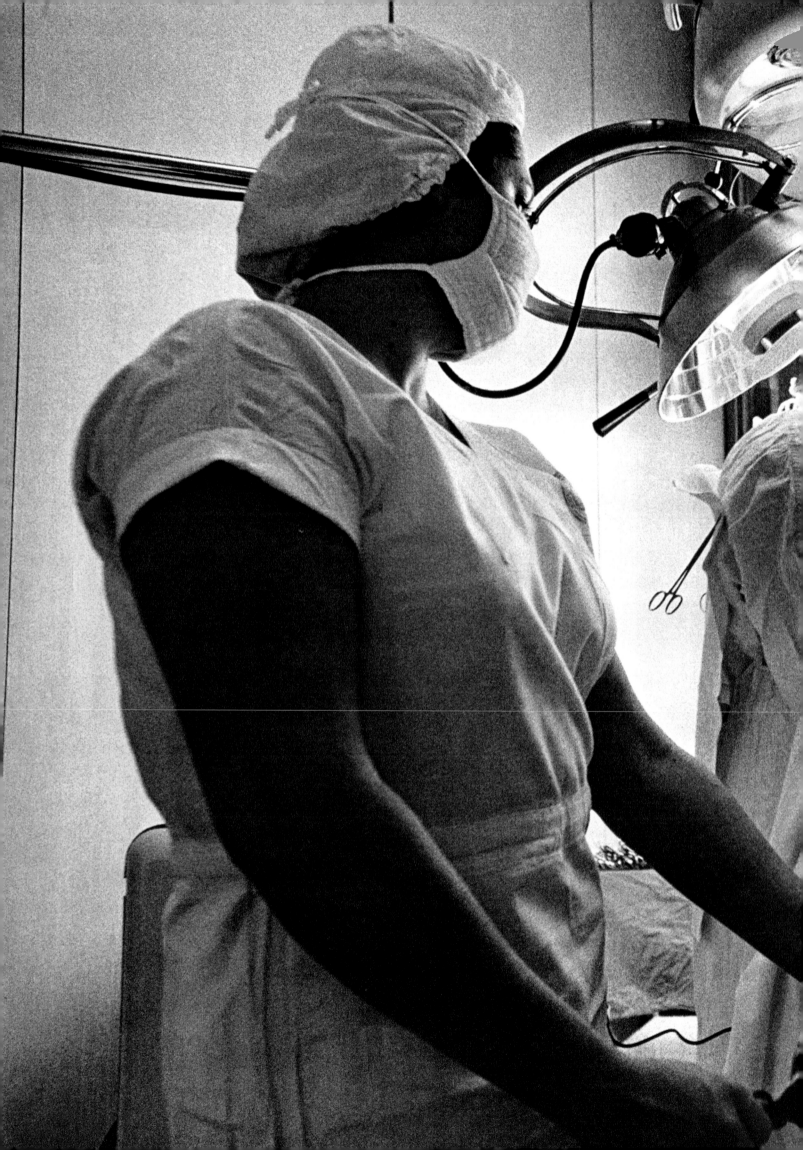

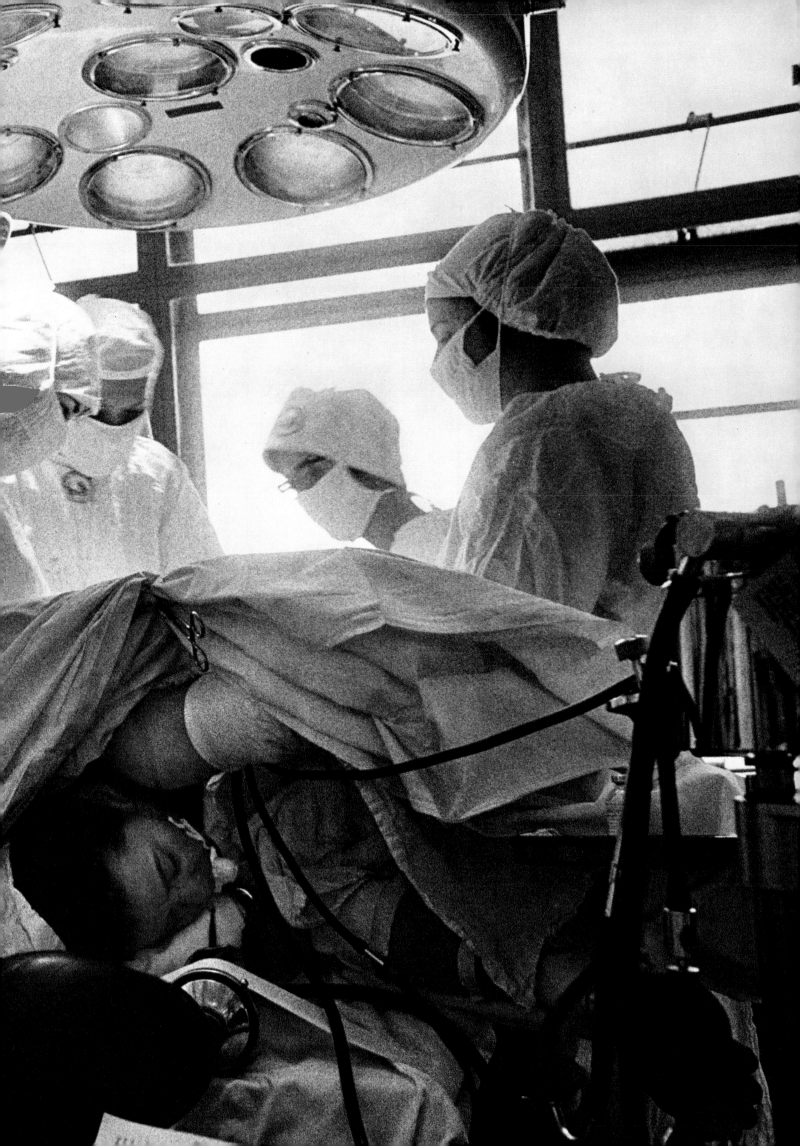

Gallery, Academy of Fine Arts

Leisure

For a city that is traditionally stuffed with homebodies, Philadelphia has scads of gadabouts. They like to play ball and watch it being played—baseball, basketball, football, golf—and they add a few embellishments like cricket and polo and rugby. They like music and support one of the great symphony orchestras of the world. But they also swing with jazz and have a passion for string bands. They like to look at art, but they also like to create it. And it's a big museum town, too. Some are filled with mummies, some with ship models; all with visitors. Then there are horses. Philadelphians ride them, watch them, own them, bet them. Some homebodies.

Young painter, Academy of Fine Arts

Ceramics student, Museum College of Art

University Museum

Rodin Museum

Academy of Natural Sciences

Pilot whale at Aqua

Old Original Bookbinder's

Lebanese restaurant, South Philadelphia

Impromptu dance at wedding

Collegiate rugby match

Penn Center skating rink

← Boy Scout pilgrimage, Valley Forge

Harness racing, Liberty Bell Par

Devon Horse Show

←Fox hunting near Malvern

Boxing match at the Arena

Wrestling at Convention Hall

Budding ballerinas

Scottish dance contest

cus big top

Intermission, Broadway-bound musical

Folk singing, Gilded Cage coffee house

Jazz at Billy Krechmer's

Latin Casino chor

◄– Academy of Music

Old Bar, Union League

Society dance at Bellevue

←– *High school band, Parkway*

Thanksgiving Day parade